Millionaire Bookkeeper

Starting at 21 - Married at 21

by

Hawkeye John

Milionaire Bookkeeper: Starting at 21 - Married at 21

by Hawkeye John

Published in the USA

Available at Amazon.com
(Paperback and Kindle versions)

More Stuff

Twitter: @byHawkeyeJohn (follow me & I'll follow you)

Facebook: facebook.com/hawkeye.john.writer (friend me)

Website & blog: hawkeyejohn.com (bookmark for updates)

Pinterest: pinterest.com/HawkeyeJohn (I'll follow you back)

Dedicated to all the hard working Bookkeepers out there.

Table of Contents

Chapter 1

The Story of Jill

Jill began her Bookkeeping career at the age of 21. Jill liked the work and felt that she was providing a valuable service. She married at 21. Her husband was also a bookkeeper. When Jill turned 33 years old, they bought a house for $200,000 cash.

Jill and her husband retired at the age of 60. She and her husband had accumulated $1,238,347 in cash and assets. They bought a $400,000 condo on the beach with cash.

At 60 years old Jill and her husband had a monthly income of $4,000 tax-free. They would continue to receive this $4,000 per month for the rest of their lives. They set up a trust. The trust would give $4,000 per month after they died to their favorite charity. The trust would keep giving this amount long after they were gone.

The rest of this book gives you a blueprint of how Jill and her husband accomplished their financial independence. The land of critical mass. Freedom!

Chapter 2

The 5 Rules to Follow

1. Give 10% of your income to your favorite charity. Why? Because it gives you the sense of abundance. It's a nice thing to do. It's giving back. In general, the more you give, the more you receive. It's giving thanks to the Higher Power. If you're a believer, it's giving thanks to God.

2. Contribute $250 every month to a Roth IRA (Individual Retirement Account). Invest this money in the Vanguard Total Stock Market Index Mutual Fund at https://investor.vanguard.com/home/. This investment has very low costs and has returned over 9% interest per year since its inception in 1992. In Jill's case, her investments returned an average of 9% interest per year. If the stock market is down, keep investing monthly. If the stock market is up, keep investing monthly.

3. Never borrow money. Pay cash for everything. Rent until you can buy it with cash.

4. Live below your means. Spend less than you make. Don't waste your hard earned money. Be frugal. Be creative. Sacrifice some luxuries now and hopefully you can enjoy them in abundance later without digging yourself into a hole.
5. Save money in your Piggy Bank for an emergency fund or an investment, such as a house.

Chapter 3

Millionaire Bookkeper: Starting at 21 -
Married at 21

Combined income per year = $48,000

Combined income per month = $4,000

- Give 10% of income to charity = $400
  per month
- Contribute $250 per month to Roth
  IRA
- Put $850 per month in Piggy Bank

**Money left over per month for expenses
and taxes = $2,500**

Portfolio at Age 21

- Roth IRA = $3,000
- Piggy Bank = $10,200

Total Portfolio Value = $13,200

Chapter 4

Age 22

Combined income per year = $50,000

Combined income per month = $4,167

- Give 10% of income to charity = $417 per month
- Contribute $250 per month to Roth IRA
- Put $1,000 per month in Piggy Bank

Money left over per month for expenses and taxes = $2,500

Portfolio at Age 22

- Roth IRA = $6,270
- Piggy Bank = $22,200

Total Portfolio Value = $28,470

Chapter 5

Age 23

Combined income per year = $52,000

Combined income per month = $4,333

- Give 10% of income to charity = $433 per month
- Contribute $250 per month to Roth IRA
- Put $1,150 per month in Piggy Bank

Money left over per month for expenses and taxes = $2,500

Portfolio at Age 23

- Roth IRA = $9,834
- Piggy Bank = $36,000

Total Portfolio Value = $45,834

Chapter 6

Age 24

Combined income per year = $54,000

Combined income per month = $4,500

- Give 10% of income to charity = $450 per month
- Contribute $250 per month to Roth IRA
- Put $1,300 per month in Piggy Bank

Money left over per month for expenses and taxes = $2,500

Portfolio at Age 24

- Roth IRA = $13,719
- Piggy Bank = $51,600

Total Portfolio Value = $65,319

Chapter 7

Age 25

Income per year = $56,000

Income per month = $4,667

- Give 10% of income to charity = $467 per month
- Contribute $250 per month to Roth IRA
- Put $1,450 per month in Piggy Bank

Money left over per month for expenses and taxes = $2,500

Portfolio at Age 25

- Roth IRA = $17,954
- Piggy Bank = $69,000

Total Portfolio Value = $86,954

Chapter 8

Age 26

Combined income per year = $58,000

Combined income per month = $4,833

- Give 10% of income to charity = $483 per month
- Contribute $250 per month to Roth IRA
- Put $1,600 per month in Piggy Bank

Money left over per month for expenses and taxes = $2,500

Portfolio at Age 26

- Roth IRA = $22,570
- Piggy Bank = $88,200

Total Portfolio Value = $110,770

Chapter 9

Age 27

Combined income per year = $60,000

Income per month = $5,000

- Give 10% of income to charity = $500 per month
- Contribute $250 per month to Roth IRA
- Put $1,750 per month in Piggy Bank

Money left over per month for expenses and taxes = $2,500

Portfolio at Age 27

- Roth IRA = $27,601
- Piggy Bank = $109,200

Total Portfolio Value = $136,801

Chapter 10

Age 28

Combined income per year = $62,000

Combined income per month = $5,167

- Give 10% of income to charity = $517 per month
- Contribute $250 per month to Roth IRA
- Put $1,900 per month in Piggy Bank

Money left over per month for expenses and taxes = $2,500

Portfolio at Age 28

- Roth IRA = $33,085
- Piggy Bank = $132,000

Total Portfolio Value = $165,085

Chapter 11

Age 29

Combined income per year = $64,000

Combined income per month = $5,333

- Give 10% of income to charity = $533 per month
- Contribute $250 per month to Roth IRA
- Put $2,050 per month in Piggy Bank

Money left over per month for expenses and taxes = $2,500

Portfolio at Age 29

- Roth IRA = $39,063
- Piggy Bank = $156,600

Total Portfolio Value = $195,663

Chapter 12

Age 30

Combined income per year = $66,000

Combined income per month = $5,500

- Give 10% of income to charity = $550 per month
- Contribute $250 per month to Roth IRA
- Put $1,750 per month in Piggy Bank

Money left over per month for expenses and taxes = $2,200

Portfolio at Age 30

- Roth IRA = $45,579
- Piggy Bank = $183,000

Total Portfolio Value = $228,579

Chapter 13

Age 31

Combined income per year = $68,000

Combined income per month = $5,667

- Give 10% of income to charity = $567 per month
- Contribute $250 per month to Roth IRA
- Put $2,200 per month in Piggy Bank

Money left over per month for expenses and taxes = $2,650

Portfolio at Age 31

- Roth IRA = $52,681
- Piggy Bank = $209,400

Total Portfolio Value = $262,081

Chapter 14

Age 32

Combined income per year = $70,000

Combined income per month = $5,833

- Give 10% of income to charity = $583 per month
- Contribute $250 per month to Roth IRA
- Put $2,200 per month in Piggy Bank

Money left over per month for expenses and taxes = $2,800

Portfolio at Age 32

- Roth IRA = $60,422
- Piggy Bank = $235,800

Total Portfolio Value = $296,222

Chapter 15

Age 33

Combined income per year = $70,000

Combined income per month = $5,833

- Give 10% of income to charity = $583 per month
- Contribute $250 per month to Roth IRA
- Put $2,200 per month in Piggy Bank
- Buy a house with cash from the Piggy Bank = $200,000

Money left over per month for expenses and taxes = $2,800

Portfolio at Age 33

- Roth IRA = $68,860
- Piggy Bank = $62,200
- House = $200,000

Total Portfolio Value = $331,060

Chapter 16

Age 34

Income per year = $70,000

Income per month = $5,833

- Give 10% of income to charity = $583 per month
- Contribute $250 per month to Roth IRA

Money left over per month for expenses and taxes = $5,000

Portfolio at Age 34

- Roth IRA = $78,057
- Piggy Bank = $62,200
- House = $200,500

Total Portfolio Value = $340,758

Chapter 17

Age 35

Income per year = $70,000

Income per month = $5,833

- Give 10% of income to charity = $583 per month
- Contribute $250 per month to Roth IRA

Money left over per month for expenses and taxes = $5,000

Portfolio at Age 35

- Roth IRA = $88,083
- Piggy Bank = $62,200
- House = $201,000

Total Portfolio Value = $351,283

Chapter 18

Age 36

Income per year = $70,000

Income per month = $5,833

- Give 10% of income to charity = $583
  per month
- Contribute $250 per month to Roth
  IRA

**Money left over per month for expenses
and taxes = $5,000**

Portfolio at Age 36

- Roth IRA = $99,010
- Piggy Bank = $62,200
- House = $201,500

Total Portfolio Value = $362,710

Chapter 19

Age 37

Income per year = $70,000

Income per month = $5,833

- Give 10% of income to charity = $583 per month
- Contribute $250 per month to Roth IRA

Money left over per month for expenses and taxes = $5,000

Portfolio at Age 37

- Roth IRA = $110,921
- Piggy Bank = $62,200
- House = $202,000

Total Portfolio Value = $375,121

Chapter 20

Age 38

Income per year = $70,000

Income per month = $5,833

- Give 10% of income to charity = $583 per month
- Contribute $250 per month to Roth IRA

Money left over per month for expenses and taxes = $5,000

Portfolio at Age 38

- Roth IRA = $123,904
- Piggy Bank = $62,200
- House = $202,500

Total Portfolio Value = $388,604

Chapter 21

Age 39

Income per year = $70,000

Income per month = $5,833

- Give 10% of income to charity = $583 per month
- Contribute $250 per month to Roth IRA

Money left over per month for expenses and taxes = $5,000

Portfolio at Age 39

- Roth IRA = $138,055
- Piggy Bank = $62,200
- House = $203,000

Total Portfolio Value = $403,255

Chapter 22

Age 40

Income per year = $70,000

Income per month = $5,833

- Give 10% of income to charity = $583 per month
- Contribute $250 per month to Roth IRA

Money left over per month for expenses and taxes = $5,000

Portfolio at Age 40

- Roth IRA = $153,480
- Piggy Bank = $62,200
- House = $203,500

Total Portfolio Value = $419,180

Chapter 23

Age 41

Income per year = $70,000

Income per month = $5,833

- Give 10% of income to charity = $367 per month
- Contribute $250 per month to Roth IRA

Money left over per month for expenses and taxes = $5,000

Portfolio at Age 41

- Roth IRA = $170,294
- Piggy Bank = $62,200
- House = $204,000

Total Portfolio Value = $436,494

Chapter 24

Age 42

Income per year = $70,000

Income per month = $5,833

- Give 10% of income to charity = $583 per month
- Contribute $250 per month to Roth IRA

Money left over per month for expenses and taxes = $5,000

Portfolio at Age 42

- Roth IRA = $188,620
- Piggy Bank = $62,200
- House = $204,500

Total Portfolio Value = $455,320

Chapter 25

Age 43

Income per year = $70,000

Income per month = $5,833

- Give 10% of income to charity = $583 per month
- Contribute $250 per month to Roth IRA

Money left over per month for expenses and taxes = $5,833

Portfolio at Age 43

- Roth IRA = $208,596
- Piggy Bank = $62,200
- House = $205,000

Total Portfolio Value = $475,796

Chapter 26

Age 44

Income per year = $70,000

Income per month = $5,833

- Give 10% of income to charity = $583 per month
- Contribute $250 per month to Roth IRA

Money left over per month for expenses and taxes = $5,000

Portfolio at Age 44

- Roth IRA = $230,369
- Piggy Bank = $62,200
- House = $205,500

Total Portfolio Value = $498,069

Chapter 27

Age 45

Income per year = $70,000

Income per month = $5,833

- Give 10% of income to charity = $583 per month
- Contribute $250 per month to Roth IRA

Money left over per month for expenses and taxes = $5,000

Portfolio at Age 45

- Roth IRA = $254,103
- Piggy Bank = $62,200
- House = $206,000

Total Portfolio Value = $522,302

Chapter 28

Age 46

Income per year = $70,000

Income per month = $5,833

- Give 10% of income to charity = $583 per month
- Contribute $250 per month to Roth IRA

Money left over per month for expenses and taxes = $5,000

Portfolio at Age 46

- Roth IRA = $279,972
- Piggy Bank = $62,200
- House = $206,500

Total Portfolio Value = $548,672

Chapter 29

Age 47

Income per year = $70,000

Income per month = $5,833

- Give 10% of income to charity = $583 per month
- Contribute $250 per month to Roth IRA

Money left over per month for expenses and taxes = $5,000

Portfolio at Age 47

- Roth IRA = $308,169
- Piggy Bank = $62,200
- House = $207,000

Total Portfolio Value = $577,369

Chapter 30

Age 48

Income per year = $70,000

Income per month = $5,833

- Give 10% of income to charity = $583 per month
- Contribute $250 per month to Roth IRA

Money left over per month for expenses and taxes = $5,000

Portfolio at Age 48

- Roth IRA = $338,905
- Piggy Bank = $62,200
- House = $207,500

Total Portfolio Value = $608,605

Chapter 31

Age 49

Income per year = $70,000

Income per month = $5,833

- Give 10% of income to charity = $583 per month
- Contribute $250 per month to Roth IRA

Money left over per month for expenses and taxes = $5,000

Portfolio at Age 49

- Roth IRA = $372,406
- Piggy Bank = $62,200
- House = $208,000

Total Portfolio Value = $642,606

Chapter 32

Age 50

Income per year = $70,000

Income per month = $5,833

- Give 10% of income to charity = $375 per month
- Contribute $250 per month to Roth IRA

Money left over per month for expenses and taxes = $5,000

Portfolio at Age 50

- Roth IRA = $408,923
- Piggy Bank = $62,200
- House = $208,500

Total Portfolio Value = $679,622

Chapter 33

Age 51

Income per year = $70,000

Income per month = $5,833

- Give 10% of income to charity = $583 per month
- Contribute $250 per month to Roth IRA

Money left over per month for expenses and taxes = $5,000

Portfolio at Age 51

- Roth IRA = $448,726
- Piggy Bank = $62,200
- House = $209,000

Total Portfolio Value = $719,926

Chapter 34

Age 52

Income per year = $70,000

Income per month = $5,833

- Give 10% of income to charity = $583 per month
- Contribute $250 per month to Roth IRA

Money left over per month for expenses and taxes = $5,000

Portfolio at Age 52

- Roth IRA = $492,111
- Piggy Bank = $62,200
- House = $209,500

Total Portfolio Value = $763,811

Chapter 35

Age 53

Income per year = $70,000

Income per month = $5,833

- Give 10% of income to charity = $583 per month
- Contribute $250 per month to Roth IRA

Money left over per month for expenses and taxes = $5,000

Portfolio at Age 53

- Roth IRA = $539,401
- Piggy Bank = $62,200
- House = $210,000

Total Portfolio Value = $811,601

Chapter 36

Age 54

Income per year = $70,000

Income per month = $5,833

- Give 10% of income to charity = $583 per month
- Contribute $250 per month to Roth IRA

Money left over per month for expenses and taxes = $5,000

Portfolio at Age 54

Roth IRA = $590,947
Piggy Bank = $62,200
House = $210,500

Total Portfolio Value = $863,647

Chapter 37

Age 55

Income per year = $70,000

Income per month = $5,833

- Give 10% of income to charity = $583 per month
- Contribute $250 per month to Roth IRA

Money left over per month for expenses and taxes = $5,000

Portfolio at Age 55

- Roth IRA = $647,132
- Piggy Bank = $62,200
- House = $211,000

Total Portfolio Value = $920,332

Chapter 38

Age 56

Income per year = $70,000

Income per month = $5,833

- Give 10% of income to charity = $583 per month
- Contribute $250 per month to Roth IRA

Money left over per month for expenses and taxes = $5,000

Portfolio at Age 56

- Roth IRA = $708,374
- Piggy Bank = $62,200
- House = $211,500

Total Portfolio Value = $982,074

Chapter 39

Age 57

Income per year = $70,000

Income per month = $5,833

- Give 10% of income to charity = $583 per month
- Contribute $250 per month to Roth IRA

Money left over per month for expenses and taxes = $5,000

Portfolio at Age 57

- Roth IRA = $775,128
- Piggy Bank = $62,200
- House = $212,000

Total Portfolio Value = $1,049,328

Chapter 40

Age 58

Income per year = $70,000

Income per month = $5,833

- Give 10% of income to charity = $583 per month
- Contribute $250 per month to Roth IRA

Money left over per month for expenses and taxes = $5,000

Portfolio at Age 58

- Roth IRA = $847,889
- Piggy Bank = $62,200
- House = $212,500

Total Portfolio Value = $1,122,589

Chapter 41

Age 59

Income per year = $70,000

Income per month = $5,833

- Give 10% of income to charity = $583 per month
- Contribute $250 per month to Roth IRA

Money left over per month for expenses and taxes = $5,000

Portfolio at Age 59

- Roth IRA = $927,889
- Piggy Bank = $62,200
- House = $213,000

Total Portfolio Value = $1,202,399

Chapter 42

Age 60

Income withdrawn tax-free from Roth IRA per year = $48,000

Tax-free income per month = $4,000

- Retire from Bookkeeping careers
- Buy a condo on the beach for $400,000 cash withdrawn tax-free from Roth IRA
- Give 10% of income to charity = $400 per month

Money left over per month for expenses and taxes = $3,600

Portfolio at Age 60

- Roth IRA = $567,447
- Piggy Bank = $62,200
- House = $213,500
- Condo on the beach = $400,000

Total Portfolio Value = $1,243,147

Chapter 43

Age 61

Income withdrawn tax-free from Roth IRA per year = $48,000

Tax-free income per month = $4,000

- Give 10% of income to charity = $400 per month

Money left over per month for expenses = $3,600

Portfolio at Age 61

- Roth IRA = $575,318
- Piggy Bank = $62,200
- House = $214,000
- Condo on the beach = $400,500

Total Portfolio Value = $1,252,017

Chapter 44

Age 62

Income withdrawn tax-free from Roth IRA per year = $48,000

Tax-free income per month = $4,000

- Give 10% of income to charity = $400 per month

Money left over per month for expenses = $3,600

Portfolio at Age 62

- Roth IRA = $583,896
- Piggy Bank = $62,200
- House = $214,500
- Condo on the beach = $401,000

Total Portfolio Value = $1,261,596

Chapter 45

Age 63

Income withdrawn tax-free from Roth IRA per year = $48,000

- Give 10% of income to charity = $400 per month

Money left over per month for expenses = $3,600

Portfolio at Age 63

- Roth IRA = $593,247
- Piggy Bank = $62,200
- House = $215,000
- Condo on the beach = $401,500

Total Portfolio Value = $1,271,947

Chapter 46

Age 64

Income withdrawn tax-free from Roth IRA per year = $48,000

Tax-free income per month = $4,000

- Give 10% of income to charity = $400 per month

Money left over per month for expenses = $3,600

Portfolio at Age 64

- Roth IRA = $603,439
- Piggy Bank = $62,200
- House = $215,500
- Condo on the beach = $402,000

Total Portfolio Value = $1,283,139

Chapter 47

Age 65

Income withdrawn tax-free from Roth IRA per year = $48,000

Tax-free income per month = $4,000

- Give 10% of income to charity = $400 per month

Money left over per month for expenses = $3,600

Portfolio at Age 65

- Roth IRA = $614,549
- Piggy Bank = $62,200
- House = $216,000
- Condo on the beach = $402,500

Total Portfolio Value = $1,295,249

Chapter 48

Age 66

Income withdrawn tax-free from Roth IRA per year = $48,000

Tax-free income per month = $4,000

- Give 10% of income to charity = $400 per month

Money left over per month for expenses = $3,600

Portfolio at Age 66

- Roth IRA = $626,658
- Piggy Bank = $62,200
- House = $216,500
- Condo on the beach = $403,000

Total Portfolio Value = $1,308,358

Chapter 49

Age 67

Income withdrawn tax-free from Roth IRA per year = $48,000

Tax-free income per month = $4,000

- Give 10% of income to charity = $400 per month

Money left over per month for expenses = $3,600

Portfolio at Age 67

- Roth IRA = $639,857
- Piggy Bank = $62,200
- House = $217,000
- Condo on the beach = $403,500

Total Portfolio Value = $1,322,557

Chapter 50

Age 68

Income withdrawn tax-free from Roth IRA per year = $48,000

Tax-free income per month = $4,000

- Give 10% of income to charity = $400 per month

Money left over per month for expenses = $3,600

Portfolio at Age 68

- Roth IRA = $654,244
- Piggy Bank = $62,200
- House = $217,500
- Condo on the beach = $404,000

Total Portfolio Value = $1,337,944

Chapter 51

Age 69

Income withdrawn tax-free from Roth IRA per year = $48,000

Tax-free income per month = $4,000

- Give 10% of income to charity = $400 per month

Money left over per month for expenses = $3,600

Portfolio at Age 69

- Roth IRA = $669,926
- Piggy Bank = $62,200
- House = $218,000
- Condo on the beach = $404,500

Total Portfolio Value = $1,354,626

Chapter 52

Age 70

Income withdrawn tax-free from Roth IRA per year = $48,000

Tax-free income per month = $4,000

- Give 10% of income to charity = $400 per month

Money left over per month for expenses = $3,600

Portfolio at Age 70

- Roth IRA = $687,020
- Piggy Bank = $62,200
- House = $218,500
- Condo on the beach = $405,000

Total Portfolio Value = $1,372,720

Chapter 53

Age 71

Income withdrawn tax-free from Roth IRA per year = $48,000

Tax-free income per month = $4,000

- Give 10% of income to charity = $400 per month

Money left over per month for expenses = $3,600

Portfolio at Age 71

- Roth IRA = $705,651
- Piggy Bank = $62,200
- House = $219,000
- Condo on the beach = $405,500

Total Portfolio Value = $1,392,351

Chapter 54

Age 72

Income withdrawn tax-free from Roth IRA per year = $48,000

Tax-free income per month = $4,000

- Give 10% of income to charity = $400 per month

Money left over per month for expenses = $3,600

Portfolio at Age 72

- Roth IRA = $725,960
- Piggy Bank = $62,200
- House = $219,500
- Condo on the beach = $406,000

Total Portfolio Value = $1,413,660

Chapter 55

Age 73

Income withdrawn tax-free from Roth IRA per year = $48,000

Tax-free income per month = $4,000

- Give 10% of income to charity = $400 per month

Money left over per month for expenses = $3,600

Portfolio at Age 73

- Roth IRA = $748,096
- Piggy Bank = $62,200
- House = $220,000
- Condo on the beach = $406,500

Total Portfolio Value = $1,436,796

Chapter 56

Age 74

Income withdrawn tax-free from Roth IRA per year = $48,000

Tax-free income per month = $4,000

- Give 10% of income to charity = $400 per month

Money left over per month for expenses = $3,600

Portfolio at Age 74

- Roth IRA = $772,225
- Piggy Bank = $62,200
- House = $220,500
- Condo on the beach = $407,000

Total Portfolio Value = $1,461,925

Chapter 57

Age 75

Income withdrawn tax-free from Roth IRA per year = $48,000

Tax-free income per month = $4,000

- Give 10% of income to charity = $400 per month

Money left over per month for expenses = $3,600

Portfolio at Age 75

- Roth IRA = $798,525
- Piggy Bank = $62,200
- House = $221,000
- Condo on the beach = $407,500

Total Portfolio Value = $1,489,225

Chapter 58

Conclusion

I hope this eBook has given you a snapshot of what could be. I'll repeat "The 5 Rules to Follow". Try to enjoy the journey, not just the destination.

The 5 Rules to Follow

1. Give 10% of your income to your favorite charity. Why? Because it gives you the sense of abundance. It's a nice thing to do. It's giving back. In general, the more you give, the more you receive. It's giving thanks to the Higher Power. If you're a believer, it's giving thanks to God.

2. Contribute $250 every month to a Roth IRA (Individual Retirement Account). Invest this money in the Vanguard Total Stock Market Index Mutual Fund at https://investor.vanguard.com/home/. This investment has very low costs and has returned over 9% interest per year since its inception in 1992. In Jill's case, her investments returned an average of 9% interest per year. If the stock market is down, keep investing monthly. If the stock market is up, keep investing monthly.

3. Never borrow money. Pay cash for everything. Rent until you can buy it with cash.

4. Live below your means. Spend less than you make. Don't waste your hard earned money. Be frugal. Be creative. Sacrifice some luxuries now and hopefully you can enjoy them in abundance later without digging yourself into a hole.

5. Save money in your Piggy Bank for an emergency fund or an investment, such as a house.

Available at Amazon.com
(Paperback and Kindle versions)

More Stuff

Twitter: @byHawkeyeJohn (follow me & I'll follow you)

Facebook: facebook.com/hawkeye.john.writer (friend me)

Website & blog: hawkeyejohn.com (bookmark for What's New)

Pinterest: pinterest.com/HawkeyeJohn (I'll follow your boards)